Contents

Introduction

Starting primary school is a major event in the life of any child, and one that can have a significant impact on parents too. Written by a parent who is also an experienced early years and primary teacher, this guide strives to encourage parents and their children to approach what is to come in the primary school years with enthusiasm rather than anxiety and concern.

This book provides comprehensive and straightforward information that will support parents as they prepare for their child's entry into the primary phase of education. It aims to demonstrate that there is not just one way to do this. The approach taken is up to individual parents but, armed with correct information and understanding of what is required, it should be possible to make the transition from home to school a calm and happy one.

Parents always like to ask children what they have been up to at school. This book aims to expand upon the things that the child says in response to this question by giving detailed information about what happens in a normal school day. This means that, during the early days, weeks, months and even years at school, parents will have a greater insight, and respond more fully to their child's comments about day-to-day events.

Once this awareness is established, parents will be able to become active partners in their child's education by providing learning opportunities at home to dovetail with school activities. All early years curricula across the UK emphasise the need to work closely in partnership with parents to help children's development and learning. Establishing home/school links is a vital part of a successful education.

> *Children learn and develop well in enabling environments, in which their experiences respond to their individual needs and there is a strong partnership between practitioners and parents and/or carers.*
>
> **Revised EYFS 04/05/12**

When does my child have to start primary school?

There is much to consider when deciding the right time for your child to start school. This chapter looks at the legal requirements as well as offering information on alternative childcare options available to allow you, the parent, to make an informed choice about when is the best time for your child to make this important move.

Legal requirements

The legal requirement in England, as laid out in the Education Act 1996 states:

> 'The parent of every child of compulsory school age shall cause him to receive efficient full-time education suitable -
>
> a) to his age, ability and aptitude
>
> b) to any special educational needs he may have, either by regular attendance at a school or otherwise.'

This statement has implications on your choice of how and where to educate your child as well as your ongoing rights as a parent when it comes to the education that a school should be providing your child (if a school is your choice).

The legal requirement also states that a child must start full time education by the beginning of the term following their fifth birthday. However, as of September 2011, all schools in England are also required to offer parents a place for their child from the September after the child's fourth birthday.

What this actually means is that, if you feel that in the September after your child's fourth birthday they are ready to enter the school system they will be allowed to do so, if a place is available. However, if you (the parent and expert on your own child) feel that for whatever reason your child is not quite ready, be it socially, emotionally or otherwise, then you have the right to defer your child's place until you feel they are ready, up to and including the start of the term after their fifth birthday.

Whether you are looking to defer or not you will have to apply for a school place at the usual time. Applying for a school place before the autumn of the academic year in which a child is four makes it more likely that this application will be considered.

Local authorities differ in their admissions criteria and timescales so visiting their websites or contacting them by telephone is useful. Ideally, an early application is best as most local authorities have a cut off deadline for admissions around the middle of January prior to the child starting. If you do decide to defer your child's place, then speak to the Headteacher of the school where the place has been offered as it may be possible to negotiate for your child to attend part-time until it is felt that he/she is ready for a full time place.

A word of warning

Just because your child is already attending a nursery class attached to or run by the chosen school that does not make you automatically eligible for a place in the reception class. Application for a school place needs to be made separately.

What if I choose not to send my child to a school at four?

If you choose *not* to start your child at school at four years old, there are a number of options available which may be more suited to your child's individual needs and there may be funding available from the government to help with the cost. In 2012 three and four-year olds are currently entitled to 15 hours of free education provision per week.

Possible options:

Keeping a child at home

It is possible to keep children at home until parents feel they are ready for school. The rest of this book provides ideas for learning opportunities parents can offer their children to help their ongoing development and learning in preparation for entry into the formal education system.

Pre-schools/Playgroups

These establishments are often run by a parent committee and follow the same Early Years Foundation Stage (EYFS) framework as private nurseries, and nursery and reception classes in schools. Attending such an establishment may provide a more flexible way of using the 15 hours free education which all children of this age are entitled to, for example, a child may attend for two and a half days instead of the usual five morning sessions offered by many nursery classes.

Another advantage of pre-schools and playgroups is that children can often mix with a wider range of age groups. Each child is allocated a keyworker who is responsible for liaising with parents or carers to ensure that the welfare and educational needs of the child are met through the establishment of a strong partnership.

Private Nurseries/Daycare Providers

These settings are commercial businesses, often privately owned, where children can attend from a very early age (birth upwards). Children are provided with a range of play opportunities, often in small age or ability groups. The permanent nature of these settings means that they usually offer and develop less formal environments which reflect the home, making transition into learning and education a smooth process. As with pre-schools and playgroups, these establishments provide learning opportunities that encourage children to achieve the requirements of the EYFS framework as well as delivering keyworker systems to ensure home/nursery continuity. Ratios of adults to children are formally set by the government so that there are often more adults per group of children than can be found in a school reception class.

Childminders

Childminders provide a very personalised approach to childcare, often within their own homes. They are also guided by the EYFS framework and offer appropriate learning and development opportunities for very small groups of children in a home environment and in the community. Many childminders will also pick up and drop off children at school, so any transition to school at a later date may be possible whilst maintaining personal care at their home before and after school hours.

School Nursery

Your local primary school may offer places within a nursery class or foundation stage unit for children aged three and four. Local schools will be able to inform parents if this is the case and advise as to the admission procedure. Attending a school nursery provides children with early experience of being within the school grounds, and sometimes buildings, and helps to familiarise them with many of the staff and older pupils. However, attending the school nursery does not give parents priority over others when applying for a reception place.

handy tip

Prior to your child's fifth birthday, making the right choices about which educational establishment is best for them is very much up to you as a parent. It should be a personal choice based upon many factors; it is not necessarily appropriate to start school at a particular time just because 'everyone else does'. Whatever the final choice, it is comforting to remember that all early years settings in England, Wales, Scotland and Northern Ireland follow frameworks which are regularly inspected to ensure that your child will be provided with high quality experiences tailored to meet their own particular needs and learning styles.

What should learning look like for a child within the EYFS?

Across the UK early years settings are all guided by a common set of guidelines and standards aimed at ensuring that children receive the highest levels of care and education. This chapter looks at the framework within England (EYFS) and shows you how its underlying principles should affect the provision in any primary school that you are considering.

In Sept 2008 the Early Years Foundation Stage (EYFS) was introduced in England to provide guidance for those working with children from birth to five years of age. Similar frameworks were also introduced in Wales, Scotland and Northern Ireland, although the ages they cover vary from region to region. In Wales the 'Foundation Phase' covers children from birth to seven years old.

The EYFS has subsequently been reviewed and a revised version came into practice in September 2012. This book refers to the EYFS in England but many of the underlying principles, and definitely the suggestions for supporting your child's learning, will be appropriate regardless of which early years framework your child follows.

The EYFS is a framework which all practitioners working with under fives have to work within to ensure best practice is delivered. As well as ensuring that every child is looked after in a safe secure environment by suitably qualified staff, the contents of the framework will also guide the experiences each child will have in their early days at school. It is worth exploring the differing sectors within the framework to read in simple terms what they entail and to provide some useful ideas about how parents can support this framework from home. (See Chapter 6).

The EYFS has four guiding themes which should shape practice in early years settings. These are:

- ✓ every child is a unique child who is constantly learning and can be resilient, capable, confident and self-assured;

- ✓ children learn to be strong and independent through positive relationships;

- ✓ children learn and develop well in enabling environments, in which their experiences respond to their individual needs and there is a strong partnership between practitioners and/or carers;

- ✓ children develop and learn in different ways. The framework covers the education and care of all children in early years provision, including children with special educational needs and disabilities.

Revised EYFS 04/05/2012

In simple terms this means that children should be provided with experiences within an inspiring learning environment which caters for their interests and which involves parents as part of the process. Parents should expect to be consulted about what is being developed to help their children. If a parent finds that this is not the case then he/she is entitled to question what is being provided and to actively insist on being part of the process.

It has long been established, therefore, that children learn best and make sense of things better through playing and exploring. This is why it is so important to provide an environment which enables each individual to find something to stimulate his/her interests. As a parent it is sometimes hard to understand how activities such as play dough or painting can be learning opportunities, and this will be explained in later chapters. Learning through play is based upon the belief that if children are excited and engaged in something then they are more likely to build on their existing knowledge.

Once children are motivated and ready to explore their surroundings, then staff encourage them to ask questions and take an active role in making decisions about what they will play with and how they will do so. Children enjoy being involved in the decision making process, in their time in early years, from something simple like 'What snack shall I choose today?' to group input on what they would like to see in a space station being built in the corner of their room.

They will not be spending much of their time sitting on a carpet or around a table being 'taught' things by a teacher, but will be actively engaged in making decisions themselves about what excites them and what holds their interest. The teacher's role in the early years is to know their children and build upon these interests to take learning forward, without the children realising that this is what is happening!

The children in early years classes will follow a programme of learning and development which targets skills around seven interrelated areas and these will be considered more fully in chapter 6 . The idea is that, whilst taking part in an exciting, engaging activity, such as following a pirate treasure map to dig for treasure, a child will be offered the opportunity to access all seven of these areas of learning, for example.

Communication and Language (talking about the map, discussing where to go and what to take, listening to instructions and following them to find the treasure as a group and listening to other children's ideas)

Personal, Social and Emotional Development (working together as a group to solve a problem and find the treasure, discussing feelings)

Physical Development (pouring sand into tiny containers and digging in the sand with spades to build muscles in hands and wrists)

Mathematics (using mathematical language such as 'heavy',' big', 'inside', 'under', counting pirate coins, sorting jewels by colours or sizes)

Literacy (reading maps, creating their own treasure maps and writing messages in bottles to float in the water tray)

Understanding the World (following and drawing maps and identifying key landscape features)

Expressive Arts and Design (role-playing as pirates and treasure hunters and designing and making maps, bottle messages and treasure boxes)

When the environment is planned around an interest like this, children are engaged in exciting play and learning as they enjoy themselves. Staff will be happy to answer questions and discuss children's learning achievements in specific areas.

Knowing what should be provided in a reception class or foundation unit for your child will help you to make an informed decision about which school to choose.

It will empower you to ask questions about provision and to make choices knowing what kind of experiences your child can expect. Remember that 'early years' is not the same as it used to be when many parents were at school and that the move away from formal learning is based upon proven best practice around the world, drawing on research and knowledge about how young children learn best.

Choosing a school

Unless you choose to educate your child at home (see Useful Information page 80) you will need to decide which primary school you wish to apply for. This is often not an easy decision and, even when you have made your choice, a place may not be available at your preferred school. It is essential to conduct some background research well before your child's fourth birthday.

When and where

The sooner you start to research local schools and gain an insight into their practices the better armed you will be by the time you are asked to fill in the admission application.

You can apply for a place at anytime, but most local authorities set a deadline for applications and this is usually in the autumn term before the September that your child is due to start school. Check your local authority admissions policy for more details on specific deadlines.

It is worth familiarising yourself with these as soon as possible to give you enough time to have a look around possible schools and to make the right decision for your child. For further information on general admissions policy you can visit **www.directgov.uk**

Do not assume that just because you live near a particular school or you have another child at the school that you will be automatically entitled to a place. Many different factors are taken into account when local authorities allocate primary school places including brothers and sisters already attending, special educational needs and geographical distance from the school.

 A word of warning

It is the local authority admissions department who allocate places not the school and hence if you do not receive an offer at your preferred school there is little the school can do about it. You will need to appeal to the local authority.

Most authorities will allow you to choose multiple schools in your admission application (usually three). Do not think that just because you only put down one school your child will get a place there! On the contrary if a place is not allocated at your first choice, and you do not put a second or third option, the local authority will make the decision for you. Make sure you have a back-up plan in place just in case.

Moving house

If you are moving to a new area and would like your child to start school there you must make contact with your new authority as soon as possible. Dependent upon the application deadline, it may be that you are required to apply via your existing local authority even if it is for a school in the new authority.

Also, early liaison with your new authority is vital as the schools nearest to your new home may already be full and you will need to ask about the alternative options (which could potentially involve being placed in a school some distance from your new home).

handy tip

Remember an Ofsted grade in isolation does not paint a full picture of a school's provision.

What to look for in a school?

Before making your application for a school place it is important to research a number of schools in your area and to settle on a short list of those you would like to visit and explore in more detail. Most schools now have comprehensive websites with details of activities, clubs, staff and policies which will give you a good insight into what to expect. They will often have details of their Ofsted inspection findings, or a link to the actual report, which is well worth reading.

Ofsted is a government agency which regularly inspects schools and reports on the standard of provision, giving a balanced view relating to strong aspects as well as those that require improvement. The report gives details of the inspector's actual findings and puts it into context, whereas comments by the school can sometimes be misleading, for example, stating that it has achieved 'Outstanding' or 'Good' from Ofsted but neglecting to mention any areas which have been identified as needing 'future development'.

Visiting potential schools

Once you have shortlisted your schools by looking at websites, reading prospectuses (available upon request from schools) and looking at the Ofsted website (see Useful Information page 64), it is time to organise a visit to the school to look around and decide whether it will be the most suitable one for your child. When organising a school visit a few things are worth bearing in mind:

- Ask if you can visit when the children are busy so that you can sense the classroom atmosphere and notice how involved the children are in their activities.

- Where ever possible try to be shown around by by the Headteacher. They will be able to explain their vision and answer your questions about the whole school.

- Do your homework so that you feel confident and know something about the school before you go. Ask questions that will give you a better understanding of what your child's experience will be like. It is important that you positively engage with whoever is showing you around rather than just be content to be given the standard guided tour with edited highlights.

Looking around a school is your chance to get a sense of the atmosphere of the school and find out about its overriding principles and plans for the future. Have a list of questions ready and be prepared to add to this list if you are told or see anything you do not understand during the visit. If a teacher uses jargon that is unfamiliar always ask for an explanation.

After the visit, if there is anything you are worried about or want to know, do not hesitate to pick up the phone or to pop into the school reception and ask. It is better to get all concerns and questions answered in advance than to be puzzled or disappointed once your child starts school.

Talking to other parents

As well as visiting the school it is worth asking parents of children who attend how they feel about the school, staff and learning opportunities provided. This is an ideal way of highlighting any local issues people may have with the school, but always be mindful that one parent may not have the same experience of a school as another so make sure you talk to several parents rather than just pay heed to one or two.

Frequently asked questions

What is the provision for daily outdoor play?

It is a legal requirement that children in early years have access to outdoor environments daily. Some schools have their own all-weather clothing for children to wear but you may be required to provide your own or at least to provide wellington boots and a spare change of clothes for messy outdoor play. Make sure you are aware if this is expected.

What provision do you have for snacks and healthy eating?

Young children get hungry mid morning and often need a snack. Find out whether the school provides fresh fruit daily. It may be part of a government initiative and receive free fruit and vegetables for the children. If this is not the case, then find out if your child can bring a snack to school and whether there are any restrictions on what they can bring, for example, healthy options only.

As well as asking about snacks it is worth investigating the school's policy on access to drinking water. Schools have to provide ongoing access to drinking water in early years and many now insist on children having water bottles with them throughout the school.

Are children expected to take part in organised PE sessions in early years?

Some schools have organised sessions and if this is the case you may need to provide suitable clothes, perhaps with a school logo. If there are certain physical activities that your child cannot take part in then you will need to ask about alternative provision during these sessions.

What is the provision for school meals?

Most schools provide a hot dinner but this needs to be checked as it is not always the case. If you plan to make up a packed lunch for your child, then you will need to ask whether there are any restrictions on what it can contain. If your child has any dietary restrictions you will need to explain these clearly and ask about how such restrictions are monitored so that everyone is fully aware of them. Most schools have a 'no nuts' policy but it is worth checking this if your child has a nut allergy.

handy tip

These are just a few questions you might like to ask when you visit to give you a better idea of what to expect the school to provide for your child. You will of course have lots of your own questions and please do not be afraid to ask. Your child's future education is in the hands of your chosen establishment so you have to be comfortable with what this school has to offer your child.

How does the school ensure that there is a strong partnership with parents?

It is essential to establish what the school has in place for you to gain insight into what your child is doing each week and whether you will have an opportunity to let the teacher know what he/she has been learning and enjoying at home. Perhaps there is a home/school diary or a parents' notice board?

What is the school's approach to hearing children read?

Find out how often your child will read to someone at school and who this will be. Sometimes teaching assistants support teachers in this so that children can read more frequently. Ideally, all children should read aloud to their teacher at least once a week so that the teacher can keep an overview of their progress. Ask whether your child will be expected to take a reading book home daily to read with you and whether this is part of a structured reading scheme.

Is there a school uniform?

You need to know whether your child will be expected to comply with school uniform whilst in the early years (in some schools this is voluntary until they reach Year 1). If uniform is available, ask what it is and where you can buy it. Schools are supposed to have a uniform policy which allows you to buy cheaper alternatives from local shops and supermarkets but many still insist on (or strongly recommend) a logoed item such as a sweatshirt or T-shirt.

Do you hold regular religious assemblies?

Many schools are associated with a particular church or religion and, although policy means that state funded schools cannot exclude children who are not active in that faith, it is worth asking if there are particular assemblies which are religion based. If this is the case and you do not wish your child to take part you need to find out about the alternative provision. Some church schools offer regular assemblies either at the local church or taken in school by a representative of the local church.

Can children bring things from home?

The EYFS states that children's interests should be taken as a starting point for their own learning. It is therefore important to establish that the school welcomes things from home that help them to understand what the children's current interests are, rather than seeks to make excuses as to why items from home should not be brought to school.

handy tip

Once your child is at school and feels the need to take something into school, make sure he/she knows that anything taken in may have to be shared with other children and may get broken. If it is taken, then make sure it is clearly labelled with your child's name. Pre-printed name stickers are ideal for this (see Useful Information page 80). You need to accept that it may not come back in one piece!)

What happens next?

Once you have applied for a school place, your local authority will notify you of their decision and allocate a school. If this is not your preferred choice then you do have the opportunity to appeal the decision. Your local authority will provide you with details of their own appeal process.

Appeals aside, once you know which school your child will be going to, there is much you can do to help to prepare them for this momentous milestone in their lives. The next chapter looks at some of the things a parent can do to make the transition as smooth and happy as possible and explains a little about why developing certain skills prior to starting school will give children a head start on their learning journey.

Before your child starts school

Over the weeks and days in the run up to your child starting at a new school there are quite a few things that you can do to help make this transition go as smoothly as possible. These things can be viewed from two different perspectives; things that teachers would like children to be able to do prior to starting school and things that will help your child feel more comfortable in the run up to the big day (Chapter 5). This chapter focuses on the former of the two and aims to provide ideas about how to begin developing these skills.

What skills should I be helping my child to develop prior to starting school?

There are a few key skills that teachers say time and again that children would find really useful as they settle into new school routines and learning. This chapter describes things that parents could be doing at home to help develop these skills and also explains why they are so important.

Broadly speaking there are three main areas of focus, all of equal importance.

1 Personal skills

2 Social skills

3 Learning skills

1 Personal skills

This is a set of skills which involves children being able to physically do something during their day in school. Try to help and encourage your child to be able to master as many of these as possible so that they can confidently take part in everyday routines and tasks.

Dressing and undressing

- Getting dressed is a skill which most parents accept as important to young children in the build up to school. Not only does it encourage independence and confidence but it also provides children with many skills that they can use as part of their play and learning, whether it's dressing up in costumes or putting on a painting apron, as well as the obvious need to be able to dress after going to the toilet or taking part in PE (physical education). Please try and encourage your child to undress themselves, as difficulties in this area can hinder the routines surrounding PE with many reception teachers using up valuable teaching time helping children to undo buttons, pull jumpers over heads and untangle feet from tights.

- As well as encouraging your child to undress themselves at bedtime, swimming or bathtime it is always useful if they can be encouraged to place their clothes in an orderly pile. No one expects them to be experts in folding clothes, but being able to put them all together and place their socks into their shoes will be a great help to the school staff and goes a long way to avoiding those annoying instances where, despite your best labelling efforts, your child loses a school jumper, T-shirt or one sock!

- Introduce dressing and undressing activities into play, for example, dressing and undressing dolls. Any toy clothing with fastenings, such as velcro, buttons and zips, that children can practice on is ideal. When choosing suitable clothes for school in these early days you can help them considerably by avoiding those with complicated fastenings.

- Encourage children to be able to read the name labels on their clothes and to recognise their own clothes amongst a pile of different clothing. This can be done in the form of a game involving taking turns to find a personal item of clothing from a mixed up pile, or by pretending to sort washing into piles for each family member. Pairing socks is an excellent way of helping children to remember which ones belong to them.

handy tip

Don't forget to try and teach your child to put on and fasten their coat as there is nothing more frustrating for a child, desperate to get outside and play, than to have to wait for an adult to come and help them put their coat on.

Toileting

The ability to use the toilet independently gives a child freedom and confidence. Most schools will insist on children being toilet trained and out of nappies before they begin to attend full-time. Many children find this difficult at four years old and parents have a key role in ensuring that any difficulties are overcome in good time.

✳ Children should be aware when they need to go to the toilet and to give themselves enough time to get there to avoid any accidents. Prior to starting school, encourage your child to do this unaided as much as possible and if you are out, for example, in a shop or park, try to take your child as soon as they ask. That way children learn that if they ask to go to the toilet they can go pretty much straight away. Asking an adult immediately is vital in a nursery or reception class so that teachers can respond before there is an accident and also be aware of where every child is. Many classrooms have toilets within them and so children can go when they please without asking. Make sure before your child starts that they know the procedure and understand whether or not they need to ask before going.

✳ When visiting the toilet children need to be able to cope with items such as buttons, zips, elastic and tights. Help your child at home with these so that they are confident about managing tricky clothing and fastenings for themselves but emphasise that they can ask for help if they get really stuck. Make things easier by considering the clothing you purchase for your child so that you avoid any really difficult fastenings.

✳ Encourage children to use toilet paper hygienically and to dispose of it in the toilet. Give plenty of positive praise for good toileting habits at home to help to make the process stress free when in school. School is probably the first place that many children will have to share toilet facilities with a number of other children, and even different classes, without the presence of an adult so the need to be able to use a toilet correctly and to flush afterwards is key to maintaining good school facilities. Encourage your child to pull the toilet flush or press the button on the toilet whilst out on a trip or at the shops. Making this part of the toileting routine will really help when they start school.

✳ Building up a good hand washing routine from a very early age will ensure hygiene is maintained at school both at toilet time, and also in preparation for snack, lunch and any baking activities they may be a part of. Develop a little chant, such as 'front and back and in between' as you do so as a good way of ensuring children cover the front and backs of their hands with both soap and water when washing. Teach children to pull up their sleeves before washing their hands to avoid soggy cuffs getting in the way of play activities.

23

Mealtime skills

By the age of four your child should be encouraged to be eating their meals with a fork or spoon (preferably both), holding them correctly to be able to feed themselves. Introducing a knife to some soft foods such as fish fingers or sausages is a good way of starting to build on this skill which they will definitely need if they are having cooked school lunches.

✳ Whether your child is having school dinners or a packed lunch, they will be expected to sit at a table to eat. Try to encourage your family to sit down together for a main meal so that your child can enjoy this special experience. This will help their independence and confidence when faced with the often noisy and seemingly chaotic scenes of school halls at lunchtime.

✳ If your child is having a packed lunch, try to prepare them for the kinds of things they might find in their lunch box. Being able to open a packet of crisps or undo a plastic food tub are skills which can make a huge difference to how easily your child can access their own food at lunchtime. There is no point in putting in a healthy satsuma if your child cannot peel it themselves! Dinner time staff are there to help, but they have to look after lots of children and can only give your child a small amount of their time on any one given day.

✳ Your child will be able to access drinking water throughout the school day. Many schools encourage children to have individual water bottles. If this is the case, then try to get your child familiar with drinking water from a bottle prior to starting. Water will be the drink of choice at schools and the more you can get your child used to drinking it at home the more likely they are to stay hydrated at school. Children need to stay hydrated to be able to learn properly and to allow their brains to function properly.

During dinnertime they will drink from a plastic cup and you should make sure that your child is confident in using a normal adult cup (not a beaker with a lid) before they start school. Whenever possible, teach them to pour water into a cup from a small jug as this may be the routine in the classroom for helping themselves to a drink. Apart from anything else, it helps to build on those all important independence and self-esteem skills which are so vital to early development.

handy tip

As with toileting, it is vital that children know how to wash their hands before they touch food so make this part of the home routine.

2) Social skills

This set of skills focuses on how your child interacts with other children and adults. The ability to make good social contact is a key skill for children to develop in order to explore their ideas at school, build good strong relationships and develop their self esteem.

Sharing

For some children being at school is one of the first situations when they come across the need to share equipment and/or adult time with other children. For others, being in a larger group of children can mean that they struggle with the need to share limited resources with each other, and some are simply not developmentally ready to share happily. Giving children lots of opportunities to be able to build their sharing skills will really help them to interact properly with other children when they begin school. There are lots of things that you can do with your child to help to develop this skill. Why not try some of these?

Sharing game

Board games for children are fun and as they play they are learning to share equipment and take turns.

Sharing activities

Choose things which your child likes to do such as colouring or doing jigsaw puzzles and explore them together. Make sure you positively point out that in doing these activities together your child is sharing with you.

Sharing a story

Try to make time to share a story or a book with your child. Encourage him/her to help you with the story telling process and to take turns to be the storyteller (even the youngest of children can retell their favourite story long before they can read it!).

Sharing baking

Children love to cook and as an activity it lends itself to being a shared task. Encourage your child to work as a team with you and/or any other children you have to make the final product. Take turns to weigh, mix, taste and so on.

Playing with others at home

Encourage your child to have 'play dates' where another child can visit your home to play. Encourage your child to let the visiting child share toys and personal belongings (ideally ask the parent of the child visiting to bring a couple of their toys with them so that the whole process works both ways).

◆ Leading by example is of course the best way to encourage your child to share and to know that sharing is a behaviour which is encouraged. If you have a sandwich or an apple for instance, offer to share it with your child. Play with toys which can be shared, such as Lego or building blocks, and remember to ask first if you can share them with your child. Make a point of offering to share some of your own pieces with your child.

◆ Remember to explain to your child that they do not have to share everything. They are bound to have some possessions which they want to keep safe and secure and they should not feel pressured into sharing these. If necessary, have a special box or cupboard where your child can safely place their 'precious things' prior to a child visiting to play, that way they will remain safe and secure until your child decides they would like them. Also try and judge when is a good time to encourage your child to share.

If they are obviously engrossed in their play and another child wishes to join them it may be that encouraging the other child to come back later is a more positive approach than disrupting the concentration and learning of the first child. Watch before you jump in with your 'sharing demands' to see if it really is the best thing in that situation.

Taking turns

✳ As with sharing there are lots of games you can play where taking turns is necessary. As well as many traditional board games, such as Snakes and Ladders and Ludo, more physical games such as Twister can be a fun way of learning to take turns. Encourage children to take turns in everyday activities for example 'It's your turn to brush your teeth now Luke' or 'It's your turn to come and have a bath' and so on. These activities all encourage children to understand that if they wait it will eventually be their turn.

If you really struggle over a particularly popular toy or game then why not try using an egg timer or sand timer and let children know that when the timer goes off it is time for the next person to have a turn.

Listening to instructions

✳ Young children will constantly be asked to do new things when they start school and when so much information is introduced at once it can be very daunting. Encourage your child to follow really simple instructions whilst you are out and about for example, 'Can you pass me the brush from the shelf please?' or 'Can you choose a cauliflower from over there for me please?' Always include the word 'please' in your requests, and when children follow an instruction correctly remember to praise and thank them.

Try not to make your instructions too complicated as most children struggle to be able to follow instructions if they are too complex or long, for instance, 'Can you get me your blue jumper from the drawer and bring it down here with your red trousers?'. Keep your instructions simple and children find them easy to follow and receive the positive praise they crave.

Introducing simple games such as 'Simon Says' are an exciting way to encourage your child to listen to and follow instructions.

Listening to others

- Listening to other people's views and opinions as well as to gain information is key to your child's start in school. Find lots of opportunities for your child to listen and absorb information, for example, listen to a story CD together and recount the story afterwards, listen to announcements on tannoys in supermarkets, shopping centres and train stations and discuss what has been said. Encourage your child to talk and listen to friends and relatives on the phone.

Behaviour (following rules)

- When your child starts school they will very quickly be asked to follow a range of rules governing behaviour. These may include things like not running indoors, not shouting out, washing their hands after going to the toilet, not using their hands or feet to hurt people and so on. Try to work with your child to establish a similar set of rules for your own house. Sit together and write them on a piece of paper and display the list in a prominent place, such as the kitchen door, where everyone can see it. Make sure you then reinforce your house rules of behaviour and refer back to the list, making comments such as 'Well done for not running in the house. You could have tripped over', or 'It's good that you didn't slam the door. You might have hurt your fingers.'

- It is important to remember when developing and reinforcing your rules together that you should always recall *why* you have put a rule in place, for example, 'We never run in the house because we are more likely to fall and get hurt' or 'We never climb on the furniture because it might break and we could get hurt'. Avoid the temptation of telling a child to do something without explaining why, for example, 'Wipe your feet when you come in'.

handy tip

Make sure that the rules are for everyone to follow and that the parent is no exception!

3 Learning skills

The final set of skills will really help your child to take full advantage of the learning opportunities they are likely to be offered once they are at school. This is a positive set of skills and not things children need to learn before they start. Don't be tempted to teach your child to read or write before they are ready and don't be drawn into discussions with other parents about what your child can do. All children are different and given a good set of basic learning skills they will all make progress at their own pace and in their own way. Remember what works for one child does not necessarily work for another!

Enjoying books

* Building a love of books is fundamental to young children's early development. Not only does it develop their imaginations, expose them to text and encourage them to see that words carry meaning but it also gives them a chance to enjoy precious moments with you where you can share a story together. As much as possible take some time to look at books together.

* If at all possible, join a library and visit it together to choose books on a regular basis. If this is not possible, then books are available from supermarkets, pound stores and charity shops. However, always make sure that secondhand books are in good condition – shabby books give a negative impression about the importance of such a precious learning resource. Teach your child to handle all books with care and respect.

* Choose books which fire your child's interest and imagination. There is no point in choosing books on dinosaurs if your child's real passion is sharks, or sticking to traditional stories if your child loves the stories of Peppa Pig. Take advantage of their favourite characters as an introduction to the wonderful range of books and stories that your child can share with you.

handy tip

It doesn't always have to be books - anything with text and stories in can be shared with excitement and enthusiasm. Why not try reading a comic, an annual or your newspaper together?

Lots of talking

◆ Never underestimate the benefit of talking to your child! At school they will need to talk to express their ideas, their choices and their needs. Talking is the way that children absorb new language and learn to use words themselves. However, it is also a great way of building the bond between you and increasing your child's self-esteem.

◆ Always remember to give children the opportunity to respond as you talk so that they can explore using the new words they are absorbing from you during shared conversations. Remember that for younger children it can take up to ten seconds to be able to process a question and formulate a response so do not be too eager to help them. Provide lots of opportunities for them to express the ideas they have in their heads, to tell stories as they play and to discuss situations new and old with you.

◆ Talk to your child as you go about daily tasks such as washing up, shopping or driving and point out what you are doing, what you are using or seeing. In that way you are feeding them with vocabulary and language patterns and providing them with the tools to be able to describe their world around them.

◆ Even when you are reading a story with your child, encourage them to talk about what is happening in the story and to tell you what they like or what they think might happen on the next page.

◆ Talking games are always fun for children so introduce games such as 'I spy' or 'What's this?' (you hide an object behind your back and have to describe it and see if the other person can guess what it is). Finally, lots of nursery rhymes and song singing will also help to give your child new words to use and build a sense of rhyme and language pattern.

handy tip

Encourage your child to walk alongside you as often as possible as pushing a pre-schooler in a forward facing buggy may make talking and listening really hard. Eye contact and facial expression can convey a lot of information to a child who is beginning to understand more complex language.

Building concentration

* At school your child will increasingly be required to concentrate on tasks for longer periods of time. In reception, these periods of focused teaching will be short as children of this age often have shorter concentration spans. There are some things you can do to help your child build these all important concentration skills at home. Playing board games together that take more than five minutes to finish is a good way of holding your child's attention for longer.

* Try sharing tasks such as colouring a picture of your child's favourite TV or book character or building a tall brick tower together. Children love treasure hunts so why not give them a list of things to find around the house or garden (simple pictures will help them to remember what is on the list). This approach can be used to help keep them focused as you go on a car journey or on a shopping trip around the supermarket too.

Recapping

✓ Children at school will need to be able to think about their play and learning experiences and to begin to talk about and make sense of what they have seen or done. This is a habit which is easy to begin well before they start school. Make it a habit to talk with your child about their day at teatime or at bedtime, encouraging them to recap on things they have done that day and pointing out things they really liked or disliked doing. Include yourself in these discussions with comments such as 'I really enjoyed it when we went to the park and you found the ladybird'. This skill helps children to build on their learning as each time they revisit a situation they strengthen brain connections. This is why they like to read stories over and over again or repeat familar chants and revisit the same activity or toy again and again.

Questioning

• We are often very good at asking questions of our children when they are young but we also need to be encouraging children to ask their own questions. Asking questions about the world around them is the basis to delivering early years learning and will really give your child a headstart at school. Try to answer as many of your children's questions as possible as this demonstrates how much you value their questions. Your answers then help to build their knowledge and understanding of the world around them. Try not to dismiss questions as 'silly' or with a 'just because' response.

handy tip

Remember that no-one knows all the answers and it is fine to say 'I don't know...shall we see if we can find out?'.

Recognising their own name (and surname)

✳ This is not about writing their name but knowing what it looks like. This is a great skill for your child to have before they start school so that they can recognise their own belongings and find things. It also helps them to recognise their names on labels on displays and walls in their classroom, giving them a sense of belonging and feeling part of the class.

Please note that your child does not need to be able to write their name before they begin school. Before children are able to pick up a pencil and hold it correctly, let alone control it enough to write their name, there are lots of skills they need to learn (see chapter 6). Also, if they are taught to write their name with letters that are not formed in the way the school requires, or in capitals, they will have to start from the beginning again before they can go forward at school.

✳ To encourage children to recognise their own name before starting, label their clothes and familiar objects such as bags and lunch boxes as well as pointing out their name at every opportunity. You can even make a simple snap or bingo game with your child's name and that of other people in your family 'Mummy, Daddy, Grandma, sister's name' and so on. In this way any words that children are recognising on sight, will be words that are familiar to them, and recognising words on sight is a useful early reading skill.

handy tip

All of the above are skills which will help your child to settle into the new routines of school more easily and help them to make sense of the learning opportunities available. Chapter 6 provides more ideas on how you can support this learning from home once your child has started school. It is vital at this stage that children are not pushed into formal learning situations too soon as this may have the opposite to the desired effect, making them anxious of failure and turning them off learning before they have even started.

Starting school

In the run up to your child starting school there are a few things you can be doing to make the transition as smooth and stress free as possible for both you and your child.

The term before

The school visit

At some point in the term prior to starting, both you and your child should get an opportunity to visit the class that they will be going into and to meet their teacher. For the children this usually is done as an introductory session (morning or afternoon) where they will have a chance to take part in some of the activities they will encounter when they start and also meet the children in their class. Check before these sessions to find out whether your child needs to wear school uniform (for some it's optional). Sometimes having a chance to wear their new school sweatshirt at this early stage will make them feel more like everyone else and enable them to find out what it feels like to be a pupil at 'big school' before starting properly.

There is usually a meeting for prospective parents, often after school or in the evening, when you can meet the teacher and ask any questions you may have about when your child starts school. During these meetings you should be given a school prospectus if you haven't already got one and this will provide you with lots of information about the school. You may also be given a list of the uniform requirements for the school and details of what to expect from your child's early learning experiences there.

Many schools provide information on how they intend to help children learn to read, write, and learn sounds so that you can all work together on these aspects of their education. At the meeting you should also be informed about where to buy any specific school items, such as book bags, PE bags and water bottles. If these are not available to buy there and then make sure that you put your order in early to ensure you have the items well in advance.

handy tip

Remember to buy items of clothing, such as school jumpers, in slightly larger sizes as your child will probably grow significantly between this meeting and starting school.

Make sure that you find out where to drop off your child and pick them up from and ask if your school has a second hand uniform shop. Many will organise evenings where you can buy school uniform items that are still in good condition at cheaper prices. There may be a stall at the actual meeting or at events such as the school summer fair.

The home visit

Towards the end of the previous term before your child is due to start school you may have a home visit from your child's new teacher. There is no need to be anxious about this visit. It is not to check up on you and your parenting skills, but a chance for the new teacher to get to know you and your child, and to find out about their likes and dislikes, their interests and the key people in their lives. This will mean that your child has a familiar face to welcome him/her into the classroom and help them to feel safer and more emotionally secure in the first few weeks.

Make sure you tell the teacher about any toys or characters your child is really interested in, whether they prefer to play indoors or outdoors and if they have any habits or routines during their day, for instance they may have a favourite blanket or toy they like to hold when they are feeling unsure or they may suck their fingers when they are tired. Teachers need to know this information so that they can keep an eye out and support your child as much as possible while they are with them.

handy tip

During the holidays, in the run up to the start of school, look out for school uniform items which your child will not grow out of in a few weeks and buy these now to spread the cost.

The test run

Walk or drive the journey to school at the right time in the morning and afternoon so that you are aware possible problems that might delay you on your school journey, such as bottle necks in traffic and parking issues. There is no point doing this in the holidays as the traffic is notably absent out of school term time and you may be unaware of the dramatic changes that school traffic brings. It is far better to avoid any situation that will cause undue stress to you and your child on your first day.

The month before

The bedtime routine

Start to prepare your child for the routine of school with a regular bedtime routine about a month before the big day. If you already have a routine in place you may need to look at moving the process forward a little in preparation for starting school.

Research suggests that children of three to five years need between 10-12 hours sleep a night to be able to function and learn properly at school. Deprivation of sleep can lead to behaviour issues, lack of concentration and an inability to retain information.

Ideally, your child should be in bed by 7.30pm, if not before. Try to establish this bedtime routine early and include a favourite shared story and a discussion about what they have enjoyed doing during the day. A regular established bedtime routine is comforting and necessary to help a child to cope with the physical and mental demands that starting school can bring.

The shopping trip

A few weeks before starting school, you can take your child to buy the remaining school uniform. Make this a special shared outing so that your child feels excited and confident about the forthcoming event. You might enjoy going for lunch together or buying a small treat for school. Check with the school first whether they will allow you to buy none logo specific items from local supermarkets and shops and make a list of what is expected in terms of colours and styles.

 handy tip Don't buy the uniform too early to ensure that the items you do purchase still fit properly on the first day. Children grow quickly and many articles of clothing are not necessary.

Items such as pens and pencils are usually provided in a reception class so you probably won't be asked to purchase these. However, it is always exciting to buy a new set of pencils or pens together and this will help to make your child even more excited about the prospect of learning and encourage them to pick up a pencil and start drawing. Encourage your child to write their own messages, cards, lists or letters but don't expect it to look like recognisable letters or words. What is important at this very early stage is that children enjoy picking up a pencil and making marks, and that they understand that these marks can carry meaning.

School shoes will probably have to be in black or blue and a good sturdy pair which have been fitted properly will be one of your best investments. Sometimes cheaper styles prove to be a false economy because inevitable wear and tear in the school playground means that you might need to buy more than one pair a term. Try to get your child's feet measured at least once a term as they often grow quickly in those first months at school.

As well as the obvious school uniform items such as polo shirts, trousers and skirts, now is the time to collect together all other school based items, for example, you may need to buy pilmsolls for PE. Children sometimes have difficulty putting on those with elasticated sides and so you may find Velcro fastenings are more suitable. However, check that the school does not have a policy on the type of plimsoll, for example, some schools insist that the sole is white to avoid marks on the polished floor in the school hall!

When buying coats and jackets, make sure your child can manage the fastenings, for example, some children have difficulty with toggles and zips, while others find them easy but cannot fasten buttons.

 handy tip Don't send your child in tights if they can't put them on and take them off themselves!

Your child will enjoy choosing a water bottle or lunch box as these come in many designs, often featuring a favourite character that can easily be recognised. Try to make sure that the lunch box is easy to open and close and that the water bottle has a secure lid.

Your child will be expected to be outdoors for a good deal of the day throughout the year. The government currently recommends that 50% of the learning time in early years takes place outdoors and for this your child will need appropriate clothing such as wellingtons and waterproofs. Some classes have sets of waterproofs for shared use, otherwise your school may recommend where to buy these all-in-one waterproofs at affordable prices. However, you will probably need to buy welliingtons yourself. Make sure wellingtons are labelled clearly and preferably pegged together. A wooden peg with your child's name on is a really easy way of making sure wellingtons are kept together when not being worn.

If your child's school does not have a uniform, then try to buy hard wearing clothes that are for school use only. This avoids arguments about what to wear in the morning and saves favourite clothes for home activities.

handy tip

Remember not to send your child to school in their best or designer clothes as they will inevitably get dirty and wet.

Additional useful items

A big black permanent marker pen is essential for marking bags, lunchboxes and the inside of shoes. You will probably only manage your child's initials inside shoes so make sure that your child is able to recognise their initials as well as their full name. Marking your child's initials under the tongue of their shoes will help to identify them easily and they will not get rubbed off by sweaty feet and socks, but make sure that your child knows where to look for these initials!

A shoe polish bottle with sponge applicator in the colour of your child's school shoes is useful. Children will explore their new school playground and outdoor area fully and, unless you want to be polishing shoes every day, a bottle of sponge on polish next to the front door will ensure that your child goes out in shoes that are clean and tidy.

If your child seems a little unsure about what to expect, visit the library and borrow some story books about popular characters at school. Try the following titles :

Starting school – by Janet and Allen Ahlberg

Harry and The Dinosaurs Go to School – by Ian Whybrow

I am too absolutely small for school (Charlie and Lola) by Lauren Child

Point out when other familiar characters, such as Peppa Pig, are at school in stories and books and highlight some of the fun things they get up to.

While reading the stories, try not to make a really big fuss about this milestone but equally do make time to listen to child's questions about school and try to answer any questions as honestly as you can. Remember not to impose your own views about school upon your child unless they are really positive.

The week before

Now is the time to label absolutely everything your child will be taking to school. Many schools offer advice on where to get labels for your child's clothes but it is definitely worth shopping around for a method which suits you. You can buy labels which need to be sewn on, ironed on or just stuck on. Sometimes, a combination of iron on labels for clothing and stick on labels for items such as water bottles and 'show and tell' toys is the most appropriate. See Useful Information (page 80) for some suppliers. If at all possible choose labels with pictures as well as a name so that your child can recognise not just the word but the symbol in their early reading days.

Although you may already have done this, take a walk along the route that you will cover or drive along at the right time of day. This will show you any new potential roadworks or obstacles which might mean you have to change your timings on the first day. Try and pick out some key landmarks along the journey so that during the first week you can ask questions as a fun way of engaging your child's interest, for example, 'What do you think we will pass next?'.

Invite your child to practise putting on their school uniform, and PE kit if they have one, and taking it off. Try to make this a fun activity, for example using an egg timer, and sharing a reward if the child succeeds in the given task. If necessary, explain as well as you can the term PE. It will probably be the first time that your child has heard this term but one that will be used often in school and teachers may assume that your child knows what to expect. Explain that, after changing into exercise clothes, they will be able to play lots of games and run, jump and skip about. Organise a pretend PE lesson with some dolls or soft toys and ask your child to get ready and join in. Ideally, dress and undress the toys too. The PE lesson then becomes something to look forward to rather than a situation that provokes anxiety.

Don't put too much pressure on your child as this is a week for being relaxed and minimising stress and anxiety. Avoid a countdown to the start of school which might add unnecessary pressure. This should be a time to enjoy together before formal education begins.

The day before

This is the day when you need to be answering children's last minute questions to allay any anxieties they may still have. Try to make the day as calm and relaxing as possible by picking something fun and interesting to do together but not something which will be too tiring.

Towards the end of the day check you have everything ready in the appropriate bags, including a spare set of clothes just in case your child has an accident when they are engrossed in messy play. Help your child to get their uniform out and ready and then aim to enjoy a relaxing bathtime, share a story and be in bed early ready for the exciting day ahead.

 As the week progresses start to build up your morning routine. Talk to your child about the things that they need to do in a morning and in which order. Take photographs of your child during different events in the morning routine, such as eating breakfast, getting washed, putting on clothes, brushing teeth, fastening shoes and so on. Print them and make them into cards so that you and your child can arrange them in sequence and talk about each event and what it involves.

 handy tip Try getting up at 'school time' to get children used to the earlier mornings, aim to have had breakfast and be washed and dressed by the time you plan to leave the house.

The big day

It is normal as a parent to feel nervous for your child on this day but try not to show your anxiety. Your child needs to feel happy and excited about the day ahead and seeing a smiling confident parent will really help. Try to encourage your child to eat some breakfast but don't worry if they do don't feel hungry, as they too may be a little apprehensive about the day.

Make sure you leave with time to spare so that the journey is relaxed and not rushed and you have plenty of time to get to the correct entrance prior to school starting. On their first day, and in some instances regularly, parents can enter the classroom with their children and help them to settle but do not stay too long after your child has found their way around.

When it is time to leave, try not to make too much fuss, simply give a reassuring smile and hug and confidently say 'I'll see you later' rather than indulge in a prolonged goodbye. Children like reassurance that you will come back later to get them, especially if it is a new experience to be away from you for a long period of time.

If you find your child really struggles with leaving you, then work closely with the teacher to minimise the stress for your child. One way is to put something small of yours, such as a handkerchief or hair bobble, in their pocket and tell them they can look after it until you come back to get them later. This will reassure them that you are coming back and also provide them with something to remind them of you if they miss you.

If you have to leave a slighty distressed child behind, then please fell free to phone the school after about half an hour to check that they have settled. A school will always be willing to reassure a concerned parent and this will put your mind at rest for the day so that you can go and enjoy your time.

Your first day away from your child

If you know that you are likely to feel anxious about your child starting school, then make plans to do something unusual once they have been dropped off, such as having a haircut, going swimming or meeting a friend for a coffee. This will help to distract you from worrying about your child who is probably quite happy and enjoying the exciting things on offer!

It is not unusual for young children to have a bit of an emotional wobble at the start of the day but generally they will be fine within a few minutes of being in a classroom with experienced adults who are used to working with such young children. This wobble can come at any time and so do not be alarmed if your previously settled child suddenly becomes upset at the start of the day. There are usually simple reasons behind this, such as being really tired, not feeling very well, worrying about something at home and in very rare occasions something at school. Again make sure you talk to your child's teacher to share any information about possible causes and to work together to settle your child.

Make sure your child has time to relax, rest or play after school before you have tea and start the bath and bedtime routine. They may bring home a reading book to share with you but this can wait until another time as at this stage this has already been a really busy day! A shared story before bed is a good time to have a quick recap of the day and may help your child to allay any anxieties and settle down so that they relax and have a good night's sleep.

At the end of the first day, and for the whole of their first week, your child will probably be really tired. Try not to keep asking about what they have done as children will usually volunteer information about the day's activities in their own time. If you are curious then ask 'What did you really enjoy today?' as this is less intimidating than 'What did you do today?' and is also more likely to get a response, even if that response is simply 'playtime' or 'lunchtime'!

The first week

Your child will probably be really tired during their first week with all the new experiences, early mornings and long days. Make allowances for this, and do not try to pack the time after school with too much activity, play dates or clubs as your child needs plenty of time to recharge their batteries.

handy tip

Remember that, although you have tried to prepare your child for their first day at school, each day this week will bring new experiences as your child enjoys the whole week's timetable. Try to treat each day as a first day at school.

If you have concerns or questions that have arisen during the first week try to avoid speaking to the teacher at the start of the day as that is a really busy time. Children need to be settled and get started with the activities that have been planned for that day. Waiting until the end of the day is much more suitable, and, if the teacher thinks it would be better to make an appointment to discuss any issue further, it will be easier for them when the classroom is quiet.

Don't forget that other parents may have the answers to some of your questions, or may be wondering about the same thing, so it is good to start talking to other parents of children in your child's class. However, resist the temptation to become involved in the 'What my child can and can't do' discussions that can go on in playgrounds.

Supporting learning once my child has started school

This chapter offers an insight into the types of activities you should expect your child to be taking part in at school and offers ideas on how you can support this learning at home.

What should I expect my child's learning to look like at school?

Don't expect your child to sit formally at a desk. There will be some tables in a reception class but children will be able to choose what to play with and where, for example, whether to stand at an easel painting, explore equipment in water and sand trays, sit at tables with puzzles or lie on the floor with some model dinosaurs.

Don't be surprised when your child comes home full of excitement about playing with a wide variety of toys and equipment. It may sound as if they have not been learning anything but actually a sign of a well planned play activity is one in which a child does not realise that they are learning.

Similarly, don't be worried when your child comes home dirty or wearing their spare clothes because this is a sign that they have been actively taking part in the learning environment provided. If your child does come home in school spare clothes, please wash them and return them as soon as possible.

handy tip

Schools are always desperate for spare clothes so when your child grows out of their trousers, skirts and even pants and socks please think about saving them and donating them to the early years teachers at your school.

Remember that you are the expert on your own child and your views do matter. You should not feel intimidated by teachers but work with them to ensure the best possible start for your child.

The EYFS framework asks that children be given learning experiences in seven areas of learning and development. The first three of these are known as **'Prime areas'** while the rest are known as **'Specific areas'**:

Prime areas

★ Communication and Language
★ Personal, Social and Emotional Development
★ Physical Development

Specific areas

★ Mathematics
★ Literacy
★ Understanding the world
★ Expressive Arts and Design

Your part in your child's learning

The EYFS framework stipulates that parents must be included as active partners in their child's learning, including the development and planning of this. This should go well beyond the traditional twice yearly parents' evening and there should be opportunities in place to give you the chance to add your experiences of your child's learning at home to the whole picture.

Most schools have some form of home-school diary. Please use this as a way of letting your child's teacher know if you have seen your child do something exciting at home, or if they have really enjoyed taking part in a particular activity. This two way communication with the teacher will give them something to talk to your child about and to build on at school. There will usually be some kind of parent information board too where you can discover even more about what is going on at school and how you can be a part of it.

In addition to the home-school diary, your child will have an Early Years Profile, which is an individual record of their learning in all areas in their early years. This should be available for you to look at any time so remember to ask the teacher where you can access it if this is not made obvious.

This chapter explores each area in detail and explains what you might see your child doing at school to access these areas of learning and development. It also suggests some ways that you can positively support this at home. However, it's possible for all areas of learning and development to come out of one creative activity so look out for activities such as pirate treasure hunts where children can talk, work together, make maps, count coins and tell stories to name but a few ideas (see page 12). Learning in the early years is very much rooted within play activities and sometimes it is just about seeing the learning within such activities. This chapter will highlight some of the common misconceptions and explain the thinking behind why children do things differently in early years.

Prime areas of learning and development

Communication and Language

This area of learning includes understanding questions, answering them and following instructions accurately. It introduces the tools that children need to be able to talk and interact with others, and to be able to express their own ideas, feelings and experiences. It is about expanding vocabulary so that children can use language to express their imaginations and connect factual information and ideas.

You should see...

- Lots of opportunities for your child to talk, express their views and develop their ability to interact with other children. Your child's learning environment should be rich, with an abundance of exciting objects, displays and role-play activities designed to stimulate their curiosity, encourage them to ask questions, share ideas and experiences, and discuss their likes and dislikes.

- There should be lots of singing of nursery rhymes and songs which will build self-esteem as well as introduce new vocabulary and help them to become aware of the rhythm and sound patterns of language.

You should NOT see...

- Too many adult-led activities where children spend long periods of time sitting listening without the opportunity to contribute or too many situations where children take part in large group activities. Language and communication skills develop much faster when children have an active input in small groups or in one to one situations.

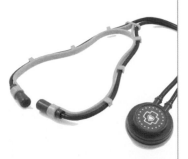

DOs

- Talk to your child at every opportunity, pointing out objects as you do the shopping, go for a walk to the park or do the cooking.

- Use the correct language rather than baby talk.

- Discuss activities you have done together, asking your child to express their likes and dislikes. Encourage your child to make choices and to verbalise them, for example, asking for a snack instead of just being given it, or telling you which pyjamas they want to wear.

- Make up stories together because imagination is a great way of exploring new words and sounds. Why not dress up and pretend to be the characters in your story together?

- Talk to your child about the stories and characters they meet in their books and ask about things they like about the story or their favourite character.

DON'Ts

- Assume that children will automatically pick up language skills. They need interaction with you, other adults and other children as well as lots of opportunities to practice their new skills.

Personal, Social and Emotional Development

This is all about developing your child's self-confidence so that they can confidently express their views and ideas and about building good relationships with other children and adults. It is also about beginning to recognise their own feelings and developing strategies for dealing with these feelings in different situations.

You should see...

- Children happily interacting with one another. This early interaction helps children to realise that not everyone shares the same views as they do and helps them to understand the need to share and take turns.

- Children moving around the room independently and following the simple rules of the classroom, for example, tidying up or hanging up an apron before leaving the messy play area.

- Teachers asking children for opinions and encouraging them to express their likes, dislikes and feelings about everyday situations and activities. By allowing them to express themselves confidently they will be building self-esteem as well as good positive mental health which has a direct impact on their physical health. Children need to know that they are unique individuals and that it is fine to be themselves no matter how different they may be.

- Children using resources they are interested in so that they can explore their own interests in the classroom. For example, a child may choose to learn numbers by counting farm animals or sort shapes by looking at *Mr Men* books. This helps children to build confidence in their teachers because they know that they have shown a personal interest in them as individuals.

You should NOT see...

- Children just being asked to point out if they feel happy, sad, angry or some other emotion without any reference to a particular situation. Children need to explore their feelings and emotions in relation to actual activities and as part of their everyday interactions with others rather than just be able to recognise happy or sad faces.

DOs

- Give your child lots of opportunities to talk about their feelings with you when they take part in activities at home. What do they really like doing? Why? What do they dislike doing? Do they like your shoes, picture, car? Let children know it is fine to have their own opinion and that it may differ from yours or that of other children.

- Talk to children about how some situations make them feel, for example, going to the dentist, the shops, swimming or birthday parties. Try not to focus on negative feelings as children need to be able to be aware of positive feelings and emotions too.

- Praise your child when they have succeeded in something, however small that triumph may be, for example, learning to ride a bike without stabilisers or being able to fasten the buttons on their shirt. Back this up by telling your child's teacher about these successes so they can reinforce these positive behaviours and achievements at school.

DON'Ts

- Encourage your child to be tough and not talk about their feelings. The very British stiff upper lip attitude which is often directed at boys can have a detrimental effect on your child's overall mental health. Mental health issues such as depression can develop in later life in individuals who have not been helped to develop skills to recognise and deal with their own feelings in a wide range of situations.

Physical Development

Physical development is key to so many other early learning skills. There is a tendency to think that it is just about running around and getting fit but it is so much more. It is about developing lots of the skills your child will need to be able to function independently and includes skills such as writing and using tools, as well as to be able to move confidently and to live healthily.

You should see...

- **Messy play**, such as play dough, sand, soap flakes or wet sawdust. These activities are designed to help with building up strong muscles in children's fingers, wrists and elbows while they have fun squishing, squashing and squeezing – these strong muscles are necessary if they are to be able to physically grip a pen or pencil later on.

- **Messy mark making** – before your child can pick up a pencil and write they need to have control over the muscles in their arms and shoulders and wrists. In early years your child will be encouraged to make marks with lots of different materials to help them to build this control. Maybe you will see them making marks in shaving foam, dry sand or jelly, or squishing freezer bags full of coloured hair gel.

- **Catching**, **kicking** and **throwing** activities as well as games that involve targets and obstacle courses, both indoors and outdoors all help to develop hand eye co-ordination and control of larger muscles (gross motor skills).

- Children need to be able to share the space around them with other children while avoiding accidents and collisions. Teachers help them to develop this ability by introducing games involving negotiating space, for example, climbing over obstacle courses or catching bubbles.

You should see...

- Indoor and outdoor activities which encourage children to develop smaller movements (fine motor skills) include threading beads onto laces, straws onto pipe cleaners or hammering nails into wood.

- You will also see lots of activities to encourage children to be able to use scissors properly. This may include cutting things other than paper such as play dough 'worms'. This sort of activity is easier than paper cutting but serves to reinforce the muscle skills in your child's hands so that eventually they are able to use a pair of scissors correctly .

- Healthy food choices are encouraged at school and many schools are part of the government's free fruit scheme. Your child may have daily access to a variety of fruits and vegetables at snack time (usually mid morning) and if not the school will probably have a policy on healthy snacks. This actively promotes healthy living and encourages your child to make healthy choices. You may also see food choices in role-play activities to encourage children to make these healthy choices as part of their ongoing imaginative play activities.

You should NOT see...

- Physical activities only being delivered as part of your child's PE lesson. Although most reception classes do have access to hall time for a group session most of their physical development happens as part of their ongoing play.

Managing personal hygiene is included in this learning area and children are encouraged to wash, dress and undress, and go to the toilet independently.

Physical Development (cont.)

DOs

- Encourage your child to build up the muscles in their hands by playing with squishy things, such as play dough, kneading bread dough or making biscuits. Allow them to play with mud and clay outdoors as well.

- Encourage your child to make marks in lots of different materials, for example, in shaving cream on the tiles while they are in the bath, with water and a paint brush on the garden fence or using chalks on the patio.

- Encourage your child to use scissors as early as possible. The more they get the chance to use them the easier it gets. Don't be afraid to let children try with 'real scissors' as they will need to get used to manipulating these heavier scissors and sometimes plastic 'children's scissors' which only cut paper can be really frustrating.

- Play lots of catching, kicking and target games together. Try throwing balls into a bucket or make skittles from old plastic drinks bottles filled with some rice and then throwing balls and bean bags at them. Playing with bats and balls of all shapes and sizes encourages the development of bigger muscle movements.

- Give your child lots of choices of fruit and vegetables and try to encourage them to make healthy choices even when out at well-known burger restaurants. However, remember that it is fine to have a treat once in a while!

- Encourage children to grow their own food. Even the smallest of windowsills can produce a harvest of salad vegetables and a small patio can support pots or grow-bags of potatoes, tomatoes, courgettes, carrots and beans.

- Encourage your child to cook with you, but not just baking so that they become familiar with fruits and vegetables, dairy products and so on. Talk to them about which foods are healthy choices.

DON'Ts

- Leave it to the school to provide your child with exercise and healthy food. Children need lots of opportunities to build their physical skills even if it is just visiting the park with a ball or walking or scooting to school.

- On the other hand do not make weekends too exhausting and packed full of activities. After a long and busy week at school your child will need some down time to recharge their batteries ready for the school week ahead. Overtired children struggle to concentrate and can be emotionally unsettled.

Specific areas of learning and development

This is not just about your child's ability to be able to write sums and do 'adding and taking away'. There are lots of skills which your child will need to develop if they are to understand and make sense of their mathematical experiences as they go through school for example, children need to be able to explore patterns, sorting, matching and shapes as well as counting.

You should see...

Patterns
Lots of opportunities for children to look for and form patterns, for example, by printing with sponges, lining up farm animals or arranging coloured bricks, beads or shapes. Mathematics is all about seeing the patterns in numbers so seeing visual patterns in real objects is a great building block for future learning.

Sorting
Lots of opportunities for children to find things that go together according to their size, shape, colour and other factors, for example, sorting a basket of fruit or some washing.

Matching
Opportunities for children to find two things which have one or more factors in common, for instance, matching pictures of their favourite characters or matching natural objects such as conkers, pine cones or leaves.

Counting

Counting consists of several different subskills:

- Being able to count in sequence
  Children will be given a wide variety of opportunities to count using the names of the numbers. Many nursery rhymes and songs use numbers in order, both forwards and backwards and including the word 'zero'. Children learn to count backwards and forwards long before they can actually count objects.

- Being able to count moveable sets of numbers
  Children will be working with lots of things that they can move as they count. This helps them to be able to count slowly and to develop an understanding of what numbers actually mean. Your child will be doing this with all sorts of things, both indoors and outdoors, including bricks, beads, toys, shapes, pebbles, balls, cars, feathers and so on.

- Being able to count non-moveable objects
  This skill comes 'after' the skill of counting moveable objects. It involves children being able to count sets of objects which are usually two dimensional and is quite difficult for young children as they have to remember which objects they have already counted and know where to stop counting. Again your child will be looking at counting using lots of sets of objects including pictures of their favourite characters, animals, vehicles and so on. Many schools then use the pictures to form number washing lines – asking children to peg the sets of numbers in order.

Simple addition and subtraction

Once children are able to count sets of objects they may be asked in their play to put two small sets of objects together and investigate how many they have altogether.

They will also be encouraged when counting to talk about how many 'one more' or 'one less' might be. Eventually they will explore taking one away to see how many are left. All of this will be done as part of ongoing fun play activities.

Recognising numbers

This comes alongside being able to count sets of objects. Children are often asked to recognise numbers on number lines and will increasingly be asked to try and match the numeral to sets of objects or to count out the correct number of objects for the numeral.

This is not done as a formal sit down lesson but may form part of a fun activity in the sand tray indoors where children count out pirate coins they have dug up or outdoors where they match pine cones to the numerals painted on pebbles.

Mathematics (cont.)

You should see...

Writing numbers

This is the same as writing letters and requires your child to be able to confidently hold and control a pencil in their hands well before they are able to form the numbers. Your child will, as with their letter formation, be encouraged to form them in lots of different materials, for example, making numbers with clay or playdough, marking numbers in wet sand with a stick or driving toy cars down a number shaped road.

Shapes

Children will be exploring lots of different shapes and starting to name them correctly. These will include all of the common two dimensional (2D) shapes, such as circles, squares, triangles and rectangles as well as 3D shapes, such as cuboids, spheres and cylinders. They will be exposed to examples of these shapes as part of games and displays as well as being encouraged to talk about the shape of items as they build with blocks or make things from empty boxes and tubes.

You should see...

Measures

Before children are able to 'measure' accurately with rulers, scales and other measuring equipment they will be given opportunities to explore what differences in length, weight or capacity (how much something holds) they notice in their play using sand, water, rice, sticks, string and so on. Children will be encouraged to use measuring language such as 'bigger, smaller, shorter, longer, heavier, lighter, full, empty' as they play with all sorts of equipment.

They will be asked to compare things according to measurements such as length, size, height and weight. They may then be encouraged to compare things using what are known as non-standard measure. For instance they may make a print of their foot in paint and then use the foot print to see how long a table or a sandpit is, making up a sentence about this such as 'The sandpit is 8 of my feet long'.

They will become familiar with measuring tools, such as tape measures and scales, as part of their imaginative play, or by weighing bags of sand or using a tape measure in the role-play building site outside.

You should NOT see...

- Your child sitting down and writing sums in exercise books or on worksheets. Remember they may not have the understanding of numbers to complete such calculations or the physical development skills to control a pencil and write numbers down. It is much more important to build the children's understanding of what 'having three' actually means than to just be able to write it.

Mathematics (cont.)

DOs

- Encourage your child to make patterns with all sorts of objects in and around your house and garden. Make patterns with children's toys, such as 'blue car', 'red car', 'blue car' and so on, or by threading chopped up bits of coloured straw or pasta tubes onto strings or pipe cleaners to show 'long', 'short', 'long', 'short'. Look for patterns when you are out walking, for example, on walls, fences, or on butterfly wings and leaves.

- Encourage children to sort their toys into sets according to colour, size or shape, for example, putting all the 'blue' cars together or finding all the 'big' Lego bricks.

- Have small storage boxes in your child's room to help them sort their toys into categories such as fairies, super heroes and so on. Try and label the boxes with a word and a picture. This will help your child when they get to school and find that all the resources are stored in drawers with word and picture labels.

- When out on a walk to school or the park, find a leaf and see if your child can find one the same shape or the same colour. Encourage your child to sort their socks into pairs with you and play matching pairs games either with shop bought sets of cards or pictures of your own printed from the computer. Play snap with your child using ordinary playing cards as this encourages matching according to colour, shape and numbers.

- Encourage your child to count with you whenever possible. Counting everyday objects really helps. Try asking your child to count three carrots for you at the shop, count the steps up to your house or tell you how many plates or forks there are on the table at teatime.

- Remember that counting objects that they can move as they count is key and can be done with just about anything. Share favourite counting rhymes and songs with your child , for example, 'Five little men in a flying saucer', 'Five little speckled frogs', 'One, two, three, four, five ... once I caught a fish alive'. Point out numerals on doors, gates, cars, buses and in shops while you are out and about.

DOs

- Encourage your child to look out for shapes while you are outdoors. Make sure you use the correct terms, for example, look for 'rectangles' on brick walls, 'squares' on paving slabs or 'circles' on the playground. Also try to use the correct 3D shape names to help your child to recognise 'spheres' in balls and bubbles, 'cylinders' in sweet packets and toilet roll tubes and 'cuboids' in cereal and toothpaste boxes. Make a collection of different shaped boxes or have some fun sorting the boxes in your recycling box.

- Picture books about shapes are ideal for naming shapes as well as boosting confidence in speaking, listening and reading skills.

- Give your child lots of chances to explore measuring around your house using a tape measure. Encourage them to use measure language such as ' The table is taller than me', 'The box is longer than the tin' and to recognise that there are numbers on rulers and measures. Even if they do not recognise them at this stage they will begin to associate measuring with numbers.

- Give your child lots of chances to play with pots, jugs, and plastic containers and bottles in both sand and water outdoors and in the bath. Introduce words like 'full', 'empty', 'heavy', 'light' while they are playing. Baking with your child helps them to see measures in practice, as they use scales to weigh out ingredients.

DON'Ts

- Spend time asking your child to write numbers before their physical pencil skills are ready, but concentrate instead on lots of counting, matching and sorting so that your child really understands what numbers are all about.

- Use commercially bought number cards to get your child to count before they can confidently count objects they can move. These will only lead to frustration when your child cannot remember where they started or decide when they should stop!

Literacy

This is not just about learning to read and write, but is also about developing a love of books and creative language. Children are encouraged to make sense of what they read and to use some of the different writing styles they encounter to inspire their own imaginative writing.

You should see...

Reading

Your child will probably bring home a reading book to share with you. In the early stages, the amount of words in these books may be minimal, and sometimes there will just be pictures. This is because it's important that your child is able to relate to the story, to be able to talk about what is happening, to predict what might happen on the next page and to simply be able to handle a book correctly, starting at the front and turning pages in the right order and direction. This reading book will probably be part of a structured reading scheme across the school and is designed to help your child progress steadily with their reading.

The process of shared reading is also designed to boost social and communication skills during this enjoyable time spent with you. Your child may also have access to a school library or book box where they are allowed to bring home a book of their own choice. In school they will have lots of opportunities to explore books, both story and fact books (fiction and non-fiction) in many areas in their classroom, for example, they may have books on trucks, diggers and tractors near the sand area or books about bugs, birds and the weather in a basket outdoors.

Your child's classroom will also have a cosy book area where children will be encouraged to regularly explore books on their own with friends or with adults. Telling your child's teacher what they like at home will ensure that the teacher can include books that will really motivate your child's interest.

As well as exposure to books all around their classroom your child will also see lots of labels around the room, for example, on equipment and displays. These are designed to help them to understand that print carries meaning and to begin to spot some common words.

Phonics

In reception, your child will probably begin to learn the sounds that some letters make (known as phonics). Your child's school should explain the approach that they use so that you can support this at home, but in general it is about helping children to recognise the actual sound of a letter, for example, 'sssssss' for the letter 's' rather than 'esss' or 'mmmm' rather than 'em' for the letter 'm'. As well as individual letter sounds your child will quickly start to explore combinations of letters (phonemes) such as 'ea''ee''ay''sh' and 'ch'. Knowing these combinations helps children to be able to take apart words that they are not sure of when reading (to decode) as well as helping them to start spelling words in their own writing. For example, the word' shop' can be broken down into three distinct sounds, 'sh' – 'o' – 'p'. Children will be exploring and building on their knowledge of letter sounds as part of their ongoing play, for example, they may be digging in the sand for things which start with the same letter sound or 'going on a sound hunt' for things beginning with a particular sound.

Word recognition

Some words are not spelt as they sound (phonetically) and need other ways to remember them. Children actually learn to read by using a combination of strategies including phonics and recognising the shape of a word. Your child's classroom should be rich in words that are not phonetically written so that they can get used to just recognising a bank of familiar words. This bank of 'on sight' words will build with exposure to more and more words. Some of the most common words (high frequency words) are 'I', 'are', 'was', 'the' and 'said'. Your child's teacher can probably provide you with a list of the words they will be using in reception so that you can support their recognition you read with your child.

Writing

There are quite a few steps leading up towards being able to write. Children need to do lots of talking, story telling, playing, sharing of ideas and exploring their thoughts before actually picking up a pencil. This will enable them to build up a strong vocabulary, an awareness of imaginative language and a clear understanding of what they actually want to write.

Literacy (cont.)

You should see...

Letter formation

Your child's school should provide you with information about how they intend to teach children correct letter formation. If they do not provide this, then ask as soon as you can. Helping your child to form letters at home in a different way from the way it's done at school can be confusing for children and have a detrimental effect on their confidence and willingness to actually try writing. These skills will be developed as part of fun play based activities, such as Jedi writing with glow sticks or fairy writing with wands (forming the letters in the air correctly). They may, as with mark making be forming letters in sand, shaving foam, mud, rice and other mixtures.

All of these activities encourage children to recognise the letter shape and to practice forming it correctly on a much larger scale than if they were just given paper and pencil. Children will then be encouraged to form letters with paint, chalks, water and paintbrushes on the ground, or with play dough or pipe cleaners. The objective is to recognise the correct formation, for example, starting at the top, and not about actually being able to pick up, hold and control a pencil.

Being an author

The process of being an author is not really about putting pen to paper, especially not in this computer age. It's really about being able to put events, people, ideas and places together to tell a story that is exciting or interesting. This is what your child will be encouraged to do through their imaginative role-play by dressing up and being a character themselves, or by playing with small world figures such as trains, dinosaurs and doll's house people to make up exciting stories.

Children playing together in the sand with some figures and making up a story together are just as much authors as J K Rowling! There is no need to be able to write it all down at this stage. It is better for your child to be able to make up imaginative stories full of exciting words than to be able to write 'I went to the shop' correctly. In this way when children have acquired all of the skills they need to be able to write what is in their heads we can be sure that what comes out of the end of a pencil is inspired and written with enthusiasm.

Writing for a reason

Children need to realise and understand that the skill of writing helps them to do particular things in life. At school they will experience lots of opportunities to write for a real reason, not just for the sake of getting some words on a page to fill up their books. They may be writing shopping lists for the supermarket role-play area, or writing out parking tickets for the drivers of the small world cars, or even creating maps or party invitations for a dramatic scenario they are acting out.

There is usually an allocated area within most early years classrooms dedicated to writing where children can access different papers and pens to write notes and messages to their friends. Remember that at this stage their writing will not look like yours but your child will be encouraged to grow in confidence. They will be inspired to have a go themselves and to value their own writing rather than to feel there is a right or wrong way to do things which could lead to a lack of confidence in their own ability, 'I can't write it, can you do it and I'll copy it?'

As well as a specific writing area your child will have access to writing materials both indoors and outdoors which they can use as part of their play. Don't be surprised to hear that your child has been writing out receipts for a car wash, writing letters to story book characters or writing messages on tree bark with chalks. It's all writing!

Putting pen to paper

Before young children can develop the skills they need to be able to confidently control a pencil to write words they need lots of opportunities to 'write' with other things. To help your child build up the correct muscles and co-ordination for pencil/pen writing on paper they may write with big marker pens, chunky chalks or just with sticks in the sand. They may use dry wipe markers to follow left to right patterns to get used to which way we write in English. Remember that other languages write from right to left or even top to bottom.

Once your child is enthusiastically picking up pencils, pens and crayons and writing with them, they will be encouraged to do so on lots of different surfaces. Writing on vertical surfaces such as white boards and blackboards helps to really strengthen the 'writing muscles' in small hands.

You should NOT see...

- Children sitting with pencils in hand being formally made to write stories or recount activities they have experienced. Also, you should not see writing for the sake of it, particularly in exercise books, but actually see your child displaying their understanding that writing is done for a reason and that writing is part of their ongoing play. You should not be seeing your child tracing over other people's writing as this can lead to a lack of confidence in their own ability to write independently and hinder the process of putting all of their exciting ideas onto paper.

DOs

- Have lots of pens, pencils and paper in different shapes, colours and textures available for your child to try writing at home. Giving them some envelopes and old Christmas or birthday cards to write on is an exciting way of encouraging them to send messages to you. Make sure you take the time to write back.

- Try writing on a different scale at home as this makes writing even more exciting. Use big chunky markers (easily available from supermarkets and pound shops) on big rolls of paper (wallpaper lining paper is readily available and much cheaper than buying purpose made rolls of craft paper). 'Post-it' notes are also really good fun for children and writing messages to each other and sticking them around the house is an excellent way of stimulating their love of writing. Chalking outside on the patio or path encourages children to explore their new writing skills and they love being able to pour water over it afterwards and mop or brush it off.

- Make sure there are lots of opportunities for your child to see you writing too. Leading by example is the best thing you can do and will show children that writing can really be a useful skill to have. Let them see you writing notes, taking messages, writing 'to do' lists and shopping lists, filling in forms and writing down dates on calendars. If they can see you writing letters then that is even better. Always have enough paper and pens to hand so that your child can join in with their own lists, notes and messages alongside you.

Literacy (cont.)

DOs

- Read as much as possible with your child. Try to find time everyday to spend at least five minutes together sharing a story or a book. Bear in mind that, after a long tiring day at school, the end of the day may not be the best time to do this. Your child may be much more responsive if you sit for five minutes in the morning and read together.

- If your child is not interested in their school reading book then, rather than force them to read it, try to read something from home which they are interested in, even if it's a comic or a newspaper. As long as you share the process, talk about what you are reading and have a go at some of the words together, the activity will be just as beneficial to your child and they are more likely to see reading as a fun way of accessing information about their favourite subjects.

- If your child continues to be uninspired by the books he/she is bringing home from school it may be worth having a word with the teacher to see if there is anything they can change. Many school reading schemes are made up of a mixture of titles from various publishers and it is usually reasonably easy to find something to interest most children.

- Instead of a bedtime story from a book every day, why not try making up your own story together sometimes? Think of characters and work together to agree what might happen to them. Encourage your child to try and think of suitable describing words to make the story even more interesting, for example, instead of starting with 'Once upon a time' why not try 'One cold, dark night...'

- Try retelling your favourite stories without the book. You might find that your child will really enjoy being able to recall the words and will become really excited if they are allowed to change the ending slightly! How exciting would it be for the Gruffalo to stay for tea with the mouse and make a cake, or for Jack to find a magical toy land at the top of his beanstalk?

- Point out common words as you read together and on signs, shops and posters when you are out and about. Children very quickly start to absorb text from their surroundings and will soon be reading things like 'bus stop', 'open', 'car park', 'cornflakes' and 'Asda'. Remember to be aware that lots of road signs are written in capital letters, for example, 'GIVE WAY' and 'SLOW' but try not to write in capital letters with your child as this just confuses them during this early stage.

DOs

- Write some really common words on paper or 'Post-it' notes and stick them to your fridge or kitchen door so children can be encouraged to have a go at reading them. You can add to and change the words as your child becomes more and more confident at recognising the words. Once they recognise a few words it is fun to mix up the words in a line to make fun sentences like 'I went up and the cat sat down'.

- If they really enjoy this approach then you can encourage them to write their own labels for items around the house, sticking labels on doors, fridges, cookers and mirrors. Remember not to worry about whether you can read it at this point. If your child can tell you what it says then that's fine and the fact that they are enjoying picking up a pen and putting it to paper should be celebrated.

- Play lots of word games with your child to encourage letter sound recognition. Variations on 'I-spy' are great for this . 'I -spy with my little eye something beginning with mmmm' or 'I-spy with my little eye something rhyming with cat'. Why not try your own variation of the famous 'Going on a bear hunt' story and go on a sound hunt, searching together for things that begin with a particular sound? How many things can you get in your collection?

DON'Ts

- Insist on your child sitting down and 'learning their letters'. Forcing children to write at an early age will supress any creative thinking or desire to write in the future.

- Get into any comparisons with other parents about what their or your child is reading. It's not a competition and every child will learn to read in their own time given access to lots of practice in the above skills. If the child feels there is too much pressure from the parent to do well then they may switch off altogether.

- Don't worry if your child does not hold a pencil correctly to begin with. It is much more important that they are happy to pick up a pen, crayon or pencil and have a go than how they hold it. The correct grip will develop over time and with practice. Using triangular shaped pens and pencils can encourage the correct grip.

Understanding the World

This area of learning involves building children's understanding of their wider world and encompasses elements of science, geography and history. It asks that children explore materials, people and places to make increasing sense of their own experiences. It also includes selecting and using technology for different purposes.

You should see...

- Lots of practical play which stimulates the senses, from messy play with mud to exploring strawberry smelling water, painting with finger paints and squidging play dough with different objects such as glitter or sequins mixed into it. These activities all encourage children to use their senses and every time your child experiences a new sensory activity they will be building new brain connections which are vital for life-long learning ability. Sensory stimulation in the early years is biologically as well as educationally the building block of future learning.

- Children asking questions and exploring their own ideas. Teachers in early years are there to listen to children and work out what interests them and then help them to explore the ideas and interests. Don't be surprised if one day your child comes home having decided to build a den for squirrels in the outdoor area, and then sporting a shield and armour the next day after being a knight for the afternoon.

- Children investigating and exploring their surroundings using scientific equipment such as magnifiers, magnets and torches. Having a fun afternoon building dens under tables and seeing what lights up inside is much more exciting, and a better way to understand aspects of light and dark, than sitting and looking at a computer programme on a whiteboard or looking at a photograph.

- A variety of pictures around the setting of children from many different cultures taking part in everyday activities. This helps all children to become aware of the cultural mix which exists in their society. If there are children who speak more than one language, expect to see labels in the home languages of these children to help them to build their reading skills in both their home language and in English.

You should see...

- Lots of chances for your child to go on supervised walks and visits to places in the immediate vicinity of the school. By visiting local businesses, landmarks and places of interest your child will build up a good understanding of their sense of being part of a much wider community.

- Evidence of children using technology as part of their everyday activities, for example, taking photographs, using a simple computer programme or playing with toys with moving parts that can be operated using switches or buttons.

✓

You should NOT see...

- Lots of worksheets for your child to fill in. Recording is only a tiny proportion of the process of scientific exploration. You should be able to view photographs of your child's explorations and read the observation notes made by a staff member to discover what your child said and what they have learned from the experience. A worksheet does not provide this evidence. It may just indicate that your child can tick boxes neatly!

- Limited nationalities and cultures represented in pictures and books in your child's classroom. Even if the school has a particular faith influence it must still provide opportunities for children to develop their awareness of other cultures and religions.

✗

Understanding the World (cont.)

DOs

- Listen to and respond to your child's questions about the world. Building on their natural curiosity is what early science is about so don't be afraid to say 'I don't know, let's see if we can find out'. You will not be expected to know all of the answers!

- Give your child exciting sensory experiences in their play at home. For example, add fruit teas or cereals to home-made play dough, or give them some spoons and bowls and ask them to help you to mix the ingredients for a cake. Letting children play with their favourite plastic toys in the bath (without batteries of course) is an excellent way of exploring floating, sinking and the pouring properties of water.

- Try and visit places which will stimulate your child to explore interesting objects and ask questions, for example, a wildlife park or the children's section of a museum. There are many such places that are free of charge or very little for entrance. A walk in the woods or to the park can be so much more interesting than a trip to the ball pool or the cinema, especially if you take a cheap magnifying glass in your pocket and a clear freezer bag to collect any exciting things you find along the way!

- Invite your child to photograph things on the way to school that really interest them. Getting children thinking and talking about their surroundings is an excellent introduction to early knowledge of geography and they will really enjoy the added responsibility of being able to use a camera. Talk to your child about the regular things they do at different times each day and across the week. This will help them to develop a sense of time in relation to their own lives.

DON'Ts

- Download and print worksheets from websites, even those that claim to be 'educational'. Exploring and understanding the world is about letting your child play and make sense of what they personally experience not simply providing them with facts and expecting them to remember them. Try looking at websites such as **The Woodland Trust** (see Useful Information on page 80) for ideas about how to enhance your child's enthusiasm and desire to find out about the surrounding natural world.

Expressive Arts and Design

This area of learning involves encouraging your child to express their thoughts and ideas through music, role-play, stories, dance and art and design.

You should see...

- A large selection of different materials that are readily available to children when they want to explore a thought or idea and represent it creatively, perhaps as a model or picture. There will probably be an area where tools and materials, such as tape, scissors and string, are kept for easy access. Ideally there will be some kind of 'creative area' where children can choose freely from a wide range of materials, such as fabric scraps, pine cones, pieces of wool and buttons.

- Lots of opportunities to explore with paint and to work with it in many states, textures, thicknesses, and colours, both indoors and outdoors. They should also be able to make tiny or huge pictures if they wish to, from small scale painting with cotton buds to extra large scale painting outdoors with mops and brooms. By exploring the many properties of paint your child will not only discover different ways of expressing their own ideas and imaginations but also begin to build on their all important physical skills. Freedom of choice helps a child to be decisive and self-confident.

- Children taking part in group singing sessions and reciting rhymes. There should be evidence of some technical equipment for playing CDs of favourite songs and rhymes that children can operate alone or with a friend. Hearing children singing or chanting as they go about their play is a sign of a good setting as this means that the musical aspect of their creativity has been actively encouraged.

You should see...

- As well as opportunities to sing, there should be easy access to instruments which your child can use to make their own sounds and music. This can be specialist multicultural instruments, such as thunder drums or rainsticks, commercial instruments such as triangles, tambourines and drums, or homemade percussion sets made from saucepans, lids and spoons. Your child should be provided with a range of resources to explore rhythm and beat.

- Lots of opportunities to explore imaginative language and story-telling through creative role-play areas on both a large and a small scale. There may be a fantasy area, such as a castle or underwater world, in the classroom or a small tray with dinosaurs and a swamp. By exploring their own ideas in these imaginative play situations your child can develop their imaginative ideas and build on their confidence to express themselves on their own and with others.

You should NOT see...

- Children being asked to copy, paint or create the same thing. A vase of sunflowers is a typical example, or a child's Christmas card that looks the same as all of the other children's cards. In early years, creativity is about giving children the skills and the tools to be able to express their own ideas not produce a perfect display for the classroom wall. Displays should show the process of learning that your child went through, perhaps by using photos and speech bubbles, as well as the final product of the learning process.

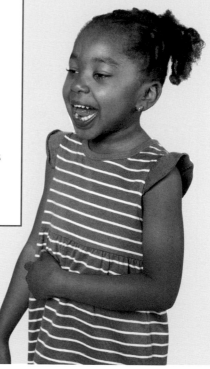

Expressive Arts and Design

DOs

- Keep your old boxes and cartons and encourage your child to explore and make things with them. Using masking tape is the best option for joining boxes together as this is easier to tear and sticks to most surfaces. Provide a small but reasonably sharp pair of scissors as well as lots of paint. Extra items such as glitter and sequins can be very exciting to use but will need careful supervision. It is best to provide small quantities and replenish them than to start with a full container.

- Help your child to use scissors from a very early age. Provide lots of scrap paper to practise on initially and gradually introduce different kinds of materials, such as card and fabric. Demonstrate how to hold and carry scissors safely with hand over the blades and handles pointing up. Be prepared to help if your child finds some items really difficult to cut but always give them time to try first.

- Sing lots of songs and rhymes with your child. Traditional rhymes are fading away but are an important part of our culture. Why not buy a book or a CD and refresh your memory?

- Encourage your child to dress up and re-enact their favourite stories as well as those that you have made up together. The stories do not always have to come out of a book and sometimes children enjoy them more if they can change the endings or add in extra characters as they wish.

- Play with puppets with your child to help build their imaginative play skills and language. Commercial puppets can often be picked up cheaply from charity shops or car boot sales, or you can make masks or puppets with card and sticks. Why not work together to put on a little show for your family or your child's friends?

- Encourage your child to 'hear' the beat of a word or a song and to tap it out on a simple drum or saucepan, or by clapping their hands. Try clapping the beats in their name or your name and then move on to favourite fruits, animals or pet names.

DON'Ts

- Try to do things for your child when they are painting or making things. If you do then all you are teaching your child is that you can do better than them and this will make them feel inadequate. Take time to encourage them and support them. It may take longer this way and the finished product may not look as pristine as if you had done it but they will be so very proud of their own achievements. Aim to build (rather than lower) their self-esteem.

- Feel frustrated if your child wants to sing the same song over and over again. Repeating something helps a child to feel secure and raises their self-confidence because they know what is coming next. They also feel a strong sense of achievement when they have mastered a song and will demonstrate this by showing their joy and enthusiasm as they sing it to others.

- Avoid letting your child explore media such as paint, clay or cutting and sticking because of potential mess. Create a safe, clean area with cheap washable tarpaulin (available cheaply from pound shops and DIY stores) and encourage your child to work within its boundaries. This will make clearing up afterwards really easy and protect your carpet at the same time.

By now it will be clear that early years at school for your child will not be the formal sit down pen to paper experience of the past, and you should understand that the learning that is going on as your child is 'playing', is part of a well planned and supervised programme of learning and development. Research has shown time and again that **taking part in play based activities is how young children learn and develop best**. This method is also used in most European countries, with many choosing not to start formal school education until children are seven years old.

The subsequent statistics for reading, writing and other subjects in these countries are amongst some of the highest in the world. Your child will hopefully benefit from this play-based approach and develop not only educationally but physically, emotionally and socially as a unique individual. As a parent never forget that you play a major part in your child's learning and development and that your child's teacher would rather you were all working together for the best outcome than pulling in different directions.

What to expect beyond the early years

Having successfully negotiated the early years your child is now ready to move forward through the school system. This chapter provides a brief summary of what to do as your child leaves reception behind and includes useful contact information to help you in your journey through primary school.

So your child has survived their first year in school, is hopefully thriving and is now about to move up to the next stage. In England the next educational stage part of school (age 5-7) is known as Key Stage 1 and incorporates Year 1 and Year 2. During these years, and for the rest of their school experience at Primary and Secondary school, your child will follow the National Curriculum which places great emphasis on both numeracy (Mathematics) and literacy (English). Your child will be expected to take part in at least one hour of literacy and numeracy based activities everyday at school. Other subjects include Science, Design and Technology, ICT (Information Communication Technology – relating to computers, all things programmable and electrically powered items), RE (Religious education), Art and Design, Physical Education, Music, History, Geography, Citizenship and Personal, Social and Emotional Health Education (PSHE).

You may notice a much more formal approach to teaching once your child enters Year 1, with more large group activities and a great deal more sitting and working at desks. Your child may struggle with these initial adjustments, as may you if you have been used to being very much part of the planning and communication process in your child's reception year and you suddenly find yourself left in the playground as your child's teacher whisks the children away into the classroom. During this transition you can support your child and encourage them to try their best with any new routines and teaching methods whilst still providing fun play based learning experiences at home. However, if you have concerns about your child always talk to your child's teacher and try wherever possible to work together to support your child.

Your child will also probably now start to be given homework, even if it is initially just some spellings to learn each week. Try to encourage your child to do a little each day, maybe before they are able to relax and watch television or play their favourite games. Establishing a good homework routine now will save you a lot of headaches later on as the homework load increases.

The future may be bright

In 2012 the National Curriculum is under review and changes to the curriculum may include scope for teachers to be more creative in their approach to engaging children in learning so that, in effect, a more early years approach will be adopted across the whole school.

Some primary schools are already taking the leap to a 'Creative Curriculum' and children are already benefiting from some really great interactive experiences. It is therefore likely that the way your child is taught may change over the next few years, to a more creative and child-centered approach that will help to maintain your child's enthusiasm and excitement for learning.

A note from the author
Whatever the approach to future education, I hope that this book has succeeded in helping you and your child to enjoy their first weeks and months at school and has given you a few ideas about how you as a parent can support your child's earliest learning experiences. Good luck and happy playing!

Useful Information

Information on admissions and how to find your local school

England – **www.direct.gov.uk/en/parents**

Scotland – **www.educationscotland.gov.uk**

Northern Ireland – **www.deni.gov.uk**

Wales – **www.wales.gov.uk/topics/ educationandskills**

Admissions in Wales are handled by individual local councils.

General curriculum information

www.early-education.org.uk – contains loads of information for parents about how best to support their child in the early years including a range of downloadable parent information leaflets.

www.literacytrust.org.uk – The National Literacy Trust website has lots of information on how to support your child's reading and writing.

www.ofsted.co.uk

Home schooling information

www.education-otherwise.net

www.home-education.org.uk

Name tag suppliers

www.mynametags.com – a combination of both iron on and stick on name labels with or without a wide choice of picture symbols

www.nametag-it.co.uk – clip on nametags range

www.easy2name.com – woven name tags for sewing onto clothes

Useful early learning websites

www.bbc.co.uk/cbeebies – lots of fun games with an early learning emphasis.

www.bbc.co.uk/schools – lots of information for parents on how to support their child at school and some really nice games for children.

www.educationcity.com – an online teaching site used by some schools in the UK, it has a parent's section which you and your child can trial for free.

www.naturedectives.org.uk – the Woodland Trust website is packed full of lots of fun and exciting activities for children to do outdoors in all seasons, including plenty of free, downloadable materials.

www.mrthorne.com – fun videos to help your child get to grips with early phonics and reading skills.

www.bigeyedowl.co.uk/science – lots of practical ideas of things you can do with your child to boost their enthusiasm for early science.

www.abcdoes.typepad.com – an early years teaching blog by ex nursery school headteacher Alistair Bryce-Clegg with lots of fun activity ideas which can equally be used with your child at home.

References

Will Nixon, *'Letting Nature Shape Childhood'*, The Amicus Journal, Fall 1997